CELEBRATING THE CITY OF MOSCOW

Celebrating the City of Moscow

Walter the Educator

Silent King Books

SILENT KING BOOKS

SKB

Copyright © 2024 by Walter the Educator

All rights reserved. No part of this book may be reproduced in any manner whatsoever without written permission except in the case of brief quotations embodied in critical articles and reviews.

First Printing, 2024

Disclaimer
This book is a literary work; the story is not about specific persons, locations, situations, and/or circumstances unless mentioned in a historical context. Any resemblance to real persons, locations, situations, and/or circumstances is coincidental. This book is for entertainment and informational purposes only. The author and publisher offer this information without warranties expressed or implied. No matter the grounds, neither the author nor the publisher will be accountable for any losses, injuries, or other damages caused by the reader's use of this book. The use of this book acknowledges an understanding and acceptance of this disclaimer.

Celebrating the City of Moscow is a little collectible souvenir book that belongs to the Celebrating Cities Book Series by Walter the Educator. Collect them all and more books at WaltertheEducator.com

USE THE EXTRA SPACE TO TAKE NOTES AND DOCUMENT YOUR MEMORIES

MOSCOW

In Moscow's heart, where history breathes and weaves,

Celebrating the City of Moscow

A city rich with tales, in endless layers deep,

From ancient times where mighty tsars did rule,

To modern days where cultures blend and sweep.

Beneath the sky, both azure bright and gray,

Spreads Moscow wide, a canvas grand and bold,

Her spires touch the heavens, where birds sway,

Celebrating the City of
Moscow

And stories of the past are bravely told.

The Kremlin stands, a fortress proud and strong,

Its ruby stars alight with crimson gleam,

Within its walls, the echoes of a song,

A hymn to power, hope, and every dream.

The Red Square stretches vast, a storied plain,

Where Lenin rests and memories reside,

The whispers of revolutions softly wane,

Yet still, they stir the city's fervent pride.

St. Basil's blooms, a symphony in stone,

Celebrating the City of
Moscow

Its vibrant domes like flames against the sky,

A testament to faith, in colors shown,

A beacon bright, where dreams and prayers fly.

Moscow's streets, a labyrinth of lore,

Where every corner holds a hidden tale,

From Arbat's charm to Tverskaya's roar,

The pulse of life within each avenue's veil.

The Moskva River winds with gentle grace,

Reflecting lights that dance in endless stream,

Celebrating the City of
Moscow

Embracing bridges, pathways to embrace,

A liquid ribbon binding every dream.

In Gorky Park, the laughter freely flows,

As children play and lovers gently stroll,

Beneath the linden trees, where beauty grows,

A haven green, where hearts find ways to roll.

The Bolshoi Theatre, grandeur's timeless throne,

Where ballets leap and operas resound,

In graceful arcs, in voices' highest tone,

Art's essence pure, in Moscow's soul is found.

The metro's veins, a network underground,

A gallery of mosaics rich and bright,

In caverns deep, where daily life is bound,

A marvel in the city's constant flight.

dear Moscow, grand and free,

A city rich with life, in endless bloom,

Your spirit lives in every heart that sees

Celebrating the City of
Moscow

ABOUT THE CREATOR

Walter the Educator is one of the pseudonyms for Walter Anderson. Formally educated in Chemistry, Business, and Education, he is an educator, an author, a diverse entrepreneur, and he is the son of a disabled war veteran. "Walter the Educator" shares his time between educating and creating. He holds interests and owns several creative projects that entertain, enlighten, enhance, and educate, hoping to inspire and motivate you. Follow, find new works, and stay up to date with Walter the Educator™ at WaltertheEducator.com.

www.ingramcontent.com/pod-product-compliance
Lightning Source LLC
LaVergne TN
LVHW012049070526
838201LV00082B/3877